Soulmate of A Searchlight

MUKESH SINGH

Chennai • Bangalore

CLEVER FOX PUBLISHING
Chennai, India

Published by CLEVER FOX PUBLISHING 2025
Copyright © Mukesh Singh 2025

All Rights Reserved.
ISBN: 978-93-67075-28-9

This book has been published with all reasonable efforts taken to make the material error-free after the consent of the author. No part of this book shall be used, reproduced in any manner whatsoever without written permission from the author, except in the case of brief quotations embodied in critical articles and reviews.

The Author of this book is solely responsible and liable for its content including but not limited to the views, representations, descriptions, statements, information, opinions and references ["Content"]. The Content of this book shall not constitute or be construed or deemed to reflect the opinion or expression of the Publisher or Editor. Neither the Publisher nor Editor endorse or approve the Content of this book or guarantee the reliability, accuracy or completeness of the Content published herein and do not make any representations or warranties of any kind, express or implied, including but not limited to the implied warranties of merchantability, fitness for a particular purpose. The Publisher and Editor shall not be liable whatsoever for any errors, omissions, whether such errors or omissions result from negligence, accident, or any other cause or claims for loss or damages of any kind, including without limitation, indirect or consequential loss or damage arising out of use, inability to use, or about the reliability, accuracy or sufficiency of the information contained in this book.

1

Reeling in life

We are Manushya (Hindi word for 'human' is a combination of Manu+Shishya) which means disciple of Manu. According to legends Manu was a wise sage. If we believe the mythology, there is a wise sage in each of us, being the descendants of Manu. Because of our inherent natural tendency to explore, perhaps writing was invented because while writing the philosopher in us wakes up as we explore beyond the things we can never know otherwise. Before there were other philosophers or Rishis, they explored themselves by becoming writers. However, the writers of today are those who were readers yesterday.

It doesn't matter if we are reading just for fun or there is a philosopher inside us who wants the deepest secrets of life to be revealed, unlike the rest of the world who will probably spend their whole lives in ignorance, we can end our miseries only by reading. And we need to remind ourselves that the reader of today is the writer of tomorrow and writing was invented to go beyond and understand what everyone was looking for but could never find.

And since time acts like a teacher and flows like a river, sooner or later everyone has to wake up to the call of time so that they can swim with its flow. It is just that once time has put up a board saying 'it is too late', there is no point in waking up. As a child I read that Veda Vyasa wrote the Gita. I was curious to know why the Lord Himself chose such a profession. Acting as a guide to provide salvation to others through the teachings of the Gita is perhaps the most challenging thing. But the truth is that He is also very much bound up with this world drama like us. In this way He is no different from us. Of course He is the supreme being, who has the ability to incarnate in human form and leave the world at will, while we have to die and be reborn against our will. The Gita is not just a collection of songs sung by the Lord but it is also an ordinance to seek the ultimate goal of realizing 'I am the soul' (only animals are not bound to follow this command of the Lord and they do not need any inner motivation to attain salvation). However things are not as simple as they may seem when reading the Gita for the first time.

The Lord exhorts Arjuna to become a Karmayogi. A Karmayogi is one who performs each action with the consciousness that I am not the doer!!

Everything is happening by the will of the Lord, I am only a spectator. For a person with an intellect like Arjuna the frustrations of life may disappear in 18 days, but for others it may not happen even after 18 births because of the catch in the following teachings:

'Just remember Me and you will be untouched by suffering.'

When you focus your intellect on His point form, thinking yourself also to be a point of light, your sins burn away. There can be no doubt about this. The obstacle here is that after a meditation session the intellect starts collecting sins while wandering according to the universal law of randomness. Every one of us is a sinner who create a lot of sinful thoughts. On an average, thousands of sinful thoughts every day are waiting to be burned by God's light.. One day you get sick and tired of this cycle due to fatigue and your connection with God is broken that leaves you frustrated and dissatisfied thereafter.

'Surrender everything to me and you will come to me.'

When you are asked to surrender every possession it means everything including mind, body and intellect. The rigid consciousness of 'the body is me' has to be changed to 'the body is mine'. There is still improvement needed here. The new perception of 'the body is His' has to be developed. The mind has to be trained against its conscious will to believe 'I am the tenant-cum-trustee of the body'.

Even when we do this mental exercise every now and then – 'My beautiful mind, now you accept that God has given us this knowledge that what we consider ours is actually belongs to Him' – the mind gets derailed and the old rut takes the place of this consciousness. After all, whatever we think inside the mind is worldliness born out of ignorance, driven by chaos. The chaos of the outer world has its own flavor, it has influenced us with its powerful vibrations to such an extent that our perspective has turned inside out. Our world is now the world we live in. Our inner world that lives inside us, creates the outer world and can reorient the disorder outside towards peace. We are Brahma, the creators of our world but number wise depending upon perfection in mental drills. The powerful Brahma will influence the world at a larger scale.

The dilemma is that although this path seems impossible, we have to follow it, otherwise life will become worthless, which is perhaps even more despised than being an animal. So, as an adult, one has to move further and further on this path as time goes by, sometimes driven by constant inner turmoil and sometimes by the joy of simply walking on this path. We think the only purpose of life is to seek salvation but we must try to witness the resolution of 'I-ness' and 'mine-ness'. Each of us is a slave to our own resolution, otherwise everyone's life is made free.

Just as death is an integral part of life, similarly salvation and life are two sides of the same coin. It is the trick of our mind to load life with bondages. The only solution is to understand this trick and make yourself a witness. When life becomes dull and sad, then a person starts searching for eternal happiness. Renunciation of the world to find happiness is an effort in this direction, which has been done by sanyasis for centuries. Although renouncing on the physical level by living in seclusion in caves will be as dull and sad as living in the world. It is possible that after going through the sufferings associated with it, the desire to live a worldly life again comes back very strongly. And so running away will never be effective, because the world you are running away from lives inside the mind. Attempts to calm the mind through pranayama and asanas are like first aid for a major illness that has very deep roots inside. Meditation, yoga asanas and pranayama are like exercise and fasting, which is good for health, no doubt but this is really when you are already healthy and want to maintain that health. Whereas now there is an urgent need to save yourself from the illness by curing it. The mind and body need powerful healing medicine and diet. Live every moment with thoughts that bring joy within. By consciously maintaining the super- conscious stage inside the mind can be defined as salvation. Salvation is not the absence of bondage but acquiring the natural state of mind, an absolutely liberated state. You are then living in this world but this world no longer lives inside your head. Then you live in solitude inside the bodily ambulatory cave, roaming around in this vicious world and free from this illness.

The life of seclusion should be like the monkey-headed sadhu (Lord Mahavira) or the elephant-headed sadhu(Lord Ganesha). Mahavira has the wisdom to recognize where he fits in the scheme of things. He devotes his life to the supreme purpose of becoming the right hand of Lord Rama in establishing Ramrajya. And similarly, Lord Ganesha has the broad wisdom to play the role of nurturing others through the powers accumulated by contemplation and meditation.

When you start to move in the world with this new realization that the body is a moving cave and I am an ascetic living inside it, there is still the possibility of suffering from the disease caused by flowing in the life adopted by others. You have to live with new consciousness continuously because the moment you forget who you are, from that moment you are like others. You can no longer consider yourself detached from the worldly desires that arise in your heart. Your mind may from time to time adopt a state of super consciousness and decieve you that you are in complete and perfect state but this will be a mistake because this is beginning of the disease. The sign of illness is that your mind has soon reached an extreme state full of desires, which is the opposite of the neutral state that there is nothing to achieve in this life or beyond this life.

Ashtavakra Gita, which was narrated by sage Ashtavakra to king Janak, through which Janak could be liberated by realizing self while living a materialistic life. One has to just observe this world as a witness. Then this world itself is land of salvation. Become a witness to your mind as well considering as if this mind also belongs to someone else because the mind is actually different from you. Ashtavakra Gita makes you a philosopher by reasoning that you are like Brahm element (like God Himself) and therefore you are always pure. And Vyasa Gita makes you a lover of the Supreme Being and inspires you to become like that. However, an interesting fact is that there is a philosopher in every lover and a lover in every philosopher. What difference then does it make whether you are like the Brahm element already or you can become one. The main thing is that your subconscious mind, when in the illusion of being Brahm element itself, can unleash unfathomable bliss.

The truth is that God, despite being different from you, is closest to you because He is an alter ego and then there is no such thing as attaining Brahm and no effort is required to become Brahm.

You got into this mirage of God's mind-born creation. You, the puppet, did such deeds that your umbilical cords that brought the nourishment from above got disconnected. Your mind then got distracted by the underlying deceitful tricks and life started to seem mundane, completely devoid of invigorating joys. This is because this world, like a banyan tree, has rotted rapidly with passage of time. Invisible filth in the form of your wasteful thoughts now signal doomsday as the randomness of an already disordered world keeps on increasing.

2

Real life

The energy field of the subtle world was at its most energetic today as the Cosmic Father Shiva himself descended on the head of the Angelic Father. Also, on such a momentous day I too joined the advance party by merging my physical form into the five elements. Now the elements along with us were eagerly waiting for the signal of the time to create our new physical forms. As I saw the Angelic Father sitting in a meditative state, I was getting wonderful visions of our various forms. A four-faced form (knowledgeable form) and a four-armed form (ruling form) appeared prominently on the screen of the intellect. With this the two fathers started showing us the visions of our next physical forms which we will assume in the heavenly city which they have created with our help.

"What a big role I have got to play and I really want it to happen soon" I wished. Then I turned to look at the advance party, they were all smiling in a celebratory mood.

"I never imagined that our presence would fill the air with such excitement, as we eagerly await our turn to play the glorious role that is uniquely etched in each of our souls. According to the plot of the glorious eternal drama, some will be part of the royal families, some of the wealthy and some of the working class. I never wanted to be separated from the advance party, although I knew it was inevitable. This means that we will soon begin the journey to the Supreme

Abode and all memories will be erased once we settle into our predetermined compartments. Then since our time of incarnation and physical appearance will be quite different for each of us, we will meet in the Heavenly City without recognizing each other," I thought.

Then finally I saw an Angelic woman swinging side by side lost in her own dreams, not caring at all about what others were doing.

"She must have already seen her new physical form. Does she take the physical form in the beginning or in the middle. And will she take the physical form of a man or a woman?" I thought.

I wanted to talk to the cosmic father Shiva as I had seen the combined form (trimurti form) in front of me for the first time. But now the atmosphere was so intoxicating that it was not possible to say anything. My mind got engrossed in counting these beads of the mala which lit up the celestial world as if hundreds of moons had come together.

"Has the count really reached 16108 including me?" I said to myself.

"Have you descended to the astral realm to take us back to your land of peace, where you live? And since you are here yourself today, wouldn't it be great if you take us there with you today?" I asked Father Shiva in a whisper, which is the only possible way to communicate in the bodiless world.

Then I heard Father Shiva whispering through the Angelic father that as soon as the Angelic body dissolves into the astral realm, you will come to me taking along with you the subtle senses (mind and intellect), which will regain their perfect state. In the meantime he told me to roam around and enjoy the heaven city he had created.

And then my mind felt for the place where I was to have many excellent future births. I thought that the subtle world of light had changed into the heavenly world. I could feel that the trees were full of juicy nutritious fruits that could sustain the future world by providing energy and strength. There would be no need to cook food. I could also feel that the air with the fragrance of flowers like nectar would keep us young and happy all our lives that's why we would live till the age of 150 without seeing any disease. We would live in golden palaces studded with precious stones that would keep it illuminated day and night. Our vehicles, flying chariots, would not run on fuel but on our mental power. The climate would always be moderate, neither too hot nor too cold, there would be no floods or earthquakes or any other calamities. Perennial rivers and lakes would provide pure potable water all our lives.

Every moment the mood of the residents is so high as if they are experiencing orgasm during intercourse, although there is no awareness of intercourse there and the genitals are considered as mere urine tubes. But women after the age of seventy-five, which will be the mature age, will produce children by spiritual power by connecting with the partner through the eyes.

Then my attention went towards the advance party, which was being welcomed by the elements manifested in human form. They respectfully said to the members of the advance party, "Gurujan! Today you are heartily welcomed because you are destroyer of the empire of darkness prevailing within you. You have reconstructed the earth, sea, air, fire and sky. Time, which decides the fate, before which everyone has to bow, changes its course on your command."

"Whatever we have achieved is attributed to you , you put us forward by remaining incognito. I bow to your greatness and grandeur." I internally expressed my gratitude to the combined form (Trimurti form) of Father Shiva and Angelic Father.

3

Reel life

I kept watching for a long time and tried to follow all the thoughts arising in my mind. I was certainly surprised to see the kind of Sankalpas getting activated. A lot was happening inside me. That I reached in Nirvana land one moment and then enjoying the heavenly city the next moment. It feels like when I am in Nirvana land it is a kind of bondage, because in that universe I sit naked(like an egg inside a shell) for ages. Whereas here I can fly like a free bird and reach anywhere at will. Though these are strange types of Sankalpas, they are capable of driving away mental fatigue. I never made any effort to resist the belief that this world is a stage. That everyone is an actor and also an audience. We all know how to play our assigned roles very well. In fact, this game is designed in such a way that every actor feels new, every scene unique.

I was watching my daughter collecting toys in a box. For a few moments, the child was completely engrossed in collecting the toys in the box. I was watching her assuming that I was just observing, while the child was the doer. But when I analyzed what happened in that simple scene, I was surprised. When I looked at myself closely, I found that the entire scene was recorded in my mind, which was coming on the screen of the mind again and again, how an innocent my child is and how I should endeavor to provide everything to her. Whatever the child did, she did it just for the sake of doing and the very next moment she got engrossed in jingling the bunch of keys with the same intensity, there was no trace of the previous action on her. Therefore, the child should be called a witness and hence a non-doer. And the doer was me though I did nothing with physical limbs throughout that scene.

The tendency to live with 'I-ness' and 'mine-ness' is the weakness that entangles us in the bondage of karma. To correct this mistake, one needs to consciously have the consciousness of being a medium – I am a medium through which the cosmic power makes everything happen.

****

I was thinking about how centuries ago, before this world became a hellish world, in the semi-heavenly period, the sages maintained the world by transmitting powerful mental waves acting as medium of Lord Shiva. As the world grew old, the sages' focus shifted from this altruistic role to materialism. Today it is necessary to repeat the past to maintain the world which is filled with never-ending suffering. When unbearable sufferings engulf the world, the grossness of life is naturally disliked.

Immerged in thoughts, I walked some distance and saw an Angelic form of an old man, from whom a radiance full of white light was emanating.

"I have met you in countless previous births, I have come again to meet you. you will become my medium to establish the new age before I take you back," the Angel whispered looking at me. I could no longer restrain myself and I ran towards the Angel and he disappeared.

****

I went to my brothers. When I started telling them about my meeting with the Angelic form today, The brothers were pleasantly surprised. The brothers gestured to each other in low voices. They looked very happy, their faces were clearly glowing. The brothers interrupted me and said, "Do you know that we really believe that he met you because while living in this depressing world we have become so convinced that a miracle can happen at any moment, even when everything seems so difficult and there seems no way out of suffering."

"When I met him yesterday, I felt that even the air that blew after touching him was full of spiritual energy. But I could not ask him when will you meet again" I said regretfully.

"We don't think we have lost the chance because this is something that is already decided. We will all meet Him soon. Although we have never seen Him with our own eyes, we believe that we were born from His mind. One thought changed our destiny. We are beads of a rosary that is called the advance party. The advance party whose destiny is to be with God in the astral realm, the whole world is renewed by them,who are ruler of the heaven" the brothers reiterated the wisdom.

Hearing this I thought for a while and decided to take them to the place where I met the Angel last time. Walking together I absorbed their vibrations and everyone's energy was the same that if the Angel of light would like to meet everyone, it was just a matter of time before this could happen.

"If you have good luck and your karma of past lives is good then you can definitely meet him" I said internally.

"We feel that you have done more good karma than us in your past lives, you really have the good fortune to meet the Angel who has come from heaven." they replied internally as we waited for Angel to come.

And we meditated for about a minute, and we had a vision of an angel with an aura of bright white light around him. We could see the light spreading in all directions. And we all felt immense power under the influence of his aura.

"Why do you think I met you? Because I am your father, who was separated from all of you for centuries. Now I have come to take you home." We felt an angel speaking in a soft voice.

First meeting an angel, then hearing his voice happened like a dream at a deep subconscious level that we do not normally feel. The whole experience was very unreal from the point of view of an earthly encounter.

Neither can I understand now nor I want to understand it anymore.

Somehow I feel we got separated from each other and the subconscious mind believes that there is a place where the angels live, where he is taking us. And I am actually created to help them in creating a new world before he take us back.

"After meeting you, we feel that we have been meeting you all along, sometimes in the subtle world, in the depths of dreams." the brothers expressed their feelings. They were not really my brothers. But from the day I met them, we have a feeling of brotherhood towards each other. And the most amazing thing is that none of them was a man. But not only I but they also considered each other as brothers. They believed that they are souls who have got female bodies. And the religion of the soul is only one and that is brotherhood.

The angel replied, "I have come to fill this sorrowful world with happiness. I have come here to make it new. A new world will be born from my mind. Now you should understand that even though you have been separated from me, I will never separate from you from now till the end. Now accept that the four-faced form which appears to be that of a Gyani is yours because you see in all directions, rising above the physical level. Though you did not meet me, my mind was connected with you which brought about a complete change in the perception of your mind. Now you start realizing that you are like Brahm and your mind is the creator and you attain complete self-sovereignty. You find that the elements, currently at lower energy have started obeying you, which is symbolized by your Chaturbhuj form." Saying this, the angel father disappeared.

4

Searching for light

Am I a shudra, tamopradhaan, impure? No! If a king ever forgets that he is a king, it does not mean that he is not a king. I am Brahman, Satopradhan, pure, though I do not realize that I am a Brahman. The truth is that I am a Brahman, free, non-doer, the truth is that I was never born because I am a traveler from Nirvanadham. My mind acts here. I have not experienced any pleasure or pain here because I am the witness. The mind which is the doer has been eating the fruits of actions. I am separate from the mind because I am without ego. This mind which is egoistic is bound to the world. When I connect myself with the mind, I also feel bound to the world. The mind is like water. When it is in Nirvana Dham it is egoless. When it is here it remains egoistic because here ego is omnipresent.

Everything keeps happening and we see changes with time. Time keeps moving like a wheel and we see everything happening. The new age becomes old and the old age becomes new. Here mournings become celebrations and celebrations become mournings. Souls descend to the earth and become mortal, souls rise above the earth and become immortal. The wheel of time moves so slowly that everything seems to be stationary. The mind moves so fast that everything seems to be changing. When the mind drops the ego, then you become a witness. And when you become a witness, the mind drops all egos. Your all creations here are predestined and destiny is all your creation.

The peaceful and holy vibrations automatically transform mind into a very peaceful and blissful state. I started experiencing profound peace with the thoughts of Angelic father.

"O my child born from my mind, will you be my instrument to protect all from the destruction that is coming ? Only after completion of this task that purifies you, you will dissolve your mortal coils so that you can attain angelic form like me." He sent messages through the sky.

With the gust of wind the flowers in the garden dance and with the purification of your soul the five elements laugh. The five elements may not have come but their image appeared on my mind. I bowed up and down in front of the five elements who had taken human forms in acknowledgment and respect.

Then I felt them saying in unison "O wealthy Yogi who has taken birth from angel's mind! By your purification we regain our original form and then you merge your body in us at your will."

The Angel of death often smiles when he listens to us talking to the elements. He is the one who always stays with us like a shadow. He is timeless. He is the link between this world and the world of angels. We are the caretakers of nature and nature cares for us. When we are happy, we create nature. When we are angry, we destroy nature. Nature gives us life when it is happy. Death is its form of anger. Nature's fury brings death. The Angel of death simply does his duty as the soul-collector. He is the transporter who sends us back to the Angelic world.

The soul is always a detached observer. But when the soul is detached, a non-doer, why does the thought of detachment come to mind? The mind gets pleasure from the fulfillment of desires, so the search for pleasure increases more. Perhaps the mind tries detachment for the novelty of supreme bliss. But if the soul becomes a witness even to the desire for detachment, the soul is free at that very moment. Although effort is required to fulfill the desire for detachment, by succumbing to the desire to attain detachment, the desire for detachment disappears. Then it can be realized that detachment was never to be attained because it is the dharma of the soul.

But when you suffer a lot of mental suffering in this world, you discover how to find peace within. Suffering is the key. Do not delve into the pains of past. No pain is greater than the pain of regretting the past. Always sit in the cave of introspection and spend your life mentally churning out words of wisdom that keep you alive. You will have to face the greatest battles again and again as you discover this peace. But it will completely destroy your old world that had burdened you. Uncovering this truth is yours greatest responsibility. It is indispensable to know the true nature of existence so that you can be fearless in the final moments.

Perhaps it was my illusion that I had once met an Angel from whom bright light was emanating all around. But this illusion that he was my father was so deeply settled in my inner being that now it seemed like truth to me. I started feeling that like the Angelic father, I too am an incarnation of light. Not only this, I started feeling that the visions of my divine light form were gradually destroying my egoistic nature of mind. That Angel was none other than my own soul, which was residing as a consciousness within a mortal body.

I, who was till now full of sorrows, was strangely immersed in happiness by seeing the truth. This divine experience started inspiring me to move forward to search for the truth of the existence of the Angelic father.

In the course of solving the mysteries of life, I was faced with another mystery. I was confused about the existence or non-existence of Angelic father, who was the Tridev form of Lord Shiva.

5

Searching in light

On any occasion, devotees stand in front of the idol in any temple for darshan because the glow in the idol attracts them. The divine light inside the idol creates a very powerful energy field in the temple premises and the devotees who come for darshan feel a tremendous surge in the mind due to the effect of divine power. After experiencing the powerful vibrations, the devotees are filled with great peace and joy for some time. If the idol of Maa Durga is in the temple, then at any moment many can also have vision of the eight-armed goddess riding a majestic lion.

Devotees consider such a visions because of mercy and blessing of deities, but it is a delusion of the mind which gives the feeling of getting a vision. Devotees have so deep belief that they start seeing glimpses of their favorite God and Goddess. But sometimes, even after trying for a long time, no vision can happen. If the mind is restless, then the visualization power of the intellect does not awaken and it is impossible to have a vision. But one can get the divine experience without having a vision of deity, which works even after going out of the temple, The divine experience is happening as divine essence has been invoked into the idol. And whenever we connect to the idol, we are in fact connected to supreme spiritual energy, Godfather Shiva.

With time, as the spiritual energy waned, the search for God increased and ways of connecting with Him were invented, as evidenced by idols. But we are also energy and so is God, who exists within us and we exist in Him. We consider ourselves to be very far from Him. Because of this illusion, we kept searching for Him which is an impossible mission because we are searching for something that has never been separate from us. Also, in the process, we got scared that we do not have the capacity to handle Him. So we agreed to the hypothesis that God is a mystery and the more we try to understand Him, the more our confusion increases. But God is never something to be searched for, but He has to be felt. We can experience His presence when the idea of searching for Him vanishes from mind. But we have to keep searching until the desire to search for Him completely vanishes from us.

One day after getting frustrated after not experiencing God by any means, I said with moist eyes and trembling voice, "O Ocean of Mercy, I call out to You with great reverence in my heart. I have felt Your presence within me. Please come out of Your transcendental world and give me Your divine darshan. Now I accept that You are there to liberate me from misery and suffering. I am happy that with this realization, the ignorance that has been living within me for ages has now vanished."

Like the devotees who goes to the temple and have the vision of deity, today, I stood before the Image of God, not out of fear or pressure of some social rule but in wait of something that could shake me to the core. some time later, I felt a strong presence of something that filled my heart with joy. I had invoked the

Angelic Father. I felt the presence and could have the vision.

"How can I be the one to see the form of light today?" I thought.

"Cycle after cycle you would start to have visions when your faith in my existence become indelible," I caught the thoughts of the Angelic Father.

I was not different from the devotees. My part in the dramatic cycle of the world was not much different from that of others. The memories of the vision of light are forever imprinted in my unconscious mind and cannot be erased. The cycle of time had brought about a situation where I had to practice intensely to see the vision of Angelic Father and that vision got forever imprinted inside me.

Like divine essence is invoked in a idol of a temple, by having vision of my

Angel of light form I felt Angelic father transmitting divine powers through me. Whether it was he actually transmitting or I was simply visualising, doubts arose but my mind got quelled. I heard myself say to myself "May be someday devotees will come to know why they see what they see"

****

It is interesting to see the effect of the descent of one's light form on oneself and on the world. The experiment would yield surprising results. The effort of going to distant temples to seek blessings may come to an end. Everyone circle around a burning flame like moths. The vision of the descent of light form can be experienced by sitting in silence and using the power of imagination. After the intense experience that the divine power emanating from the Angelic Father is entering within you, divine vibrations can be emanated from your aura to create a sacred atmosphere like that of temples.

Any premise can be filled with powerful energy just by your presence. Wherever you go, people can gradually have transcendental experiences like self-realization, visions of past lives and future lives. People suffering from migraine or depression who swallow dozens of pills prescribed by their doctor every day, but do not get any relief, can start feeling light-headed. And this will happen even faster than when the divine power of the idols gradually enters the devotee and purifies him and helps him to be in peace.

While something inspired more and more refinement into scientific research as an attempt to enhance quality of life which were infact becoming a curse to humanity bringing more and more damaging side effects.

But I knew who was inspiring me. I was influenced by the one who operates this wonderful secret mechanism that works in the most unique way, who is the generator and conductor of the universe, who possesses every power. Now I wanted to feel a glow emanating from within me because the darkness outside was enveloping my mind. Now I wanted the glow of the Angelic Father within me, like a moving image, who had the invocation of the Divine Essence within him. I wanted to see that there was an Angel of light within my physical body. This Angel of light, who is a reality, who is located within the body as a witness, who will gradually go beyond the aversion to pain or the desire for pleasure.

There is a wheel in the sky that keeps rotating. Day by day it announces a new day. Night by night it announces a new night. God is always at bliss and happiness in His world waxes and wanes like the moon. The soul is always a blazing flame and its mind smiles and cries like a child. The soul that is not a witness to the mind is either sinful or virtuous. When life is lived with the awareness that the mind is a subtle part of the soul, the soul is free from its attachment because it is always pure, then the soul and mind are like water and oil, both are separate even though together. The moment this awareness is gone, the soul and mind become like milk with water, they appear to be one even when they are separate, and then the mind is felt to be affecting the soul as well. Nevertheless, what difference does it make whether the soul is burdened or the mind is burdened by the effect of karma. For a burdened mind, saving the mind from madness is our top priority. We have to take instant recourse to self awareness as well as God awareness (Rajyoga) to save our soul. And we should try to do only good deeds, although it is true that good deeds and bad deeds together make the soul to have a realisation of non-doer, just like in a cure there is no meaning of taking medicine without the presence of disease.

There are some interesting facts about locusts, which are a special species of grasshoppers. Living in a crowd changes their behavior and appearance. Whenever they come in a crowd, their serotonin level increases, and they gather in swarms and can develop wings strong enough to fly thousands of miles. We are part of that crowd which is full of lust, anger, greed, fear, ego, the seemingly invincible obstacles, but challenges increase our serotonin level, and resistance is developed which awakens our inner powers, making us invincible.

God lives in perfect union with His creation. God is not just a point of light living in the land of Nirvana, He is an ocean. We are like fish born to swim in that ocean. We restore our faith in the existence of our subtle form living inside the body and begin to see incarnations of light in others.

To be in union with one's actions is to be awakened. He who is awake even in his sleep is a Rishi. When you are listening you are just listening, when you are speaking you are just speaking, when you are eating you are just eating, when you are watching you are just watching only when the limitless energy field of God is working through you.

6

Searchlight

For one who sees Ganeshji as the incarnation of light, Ganeshji sitting on the mouse not just symbolic, the power of Ganeshji will be awakened within him. He will be a living Ganeshji, the destroyer of obstacles and the creator of fortune. But if a devotee who has practiced intensely the visions of the physical form of Ganeshji without the power of purity can't see the incarnation of light, there is no possibility of Ganeshji's powers being awakened within him.

You may immerse yourself in the gadadhari Hanumanji, the sudarshan chakradhari Vishnuji, the trishuldhaari Shankarji, but visions will depend on your faith and the power of purity. Devotion serves no purpose without purity, there is no experience, though mental powers are engaged in idol worship. Doing yoga practice with God, in true jyotirlinga form, can only purify you.

www.ingramcontent.com/pod-product-compliance
Lightning Source LLC
LaVergne TN
LVHW061604070526
838199LV00077B/7164